BOOK SOLD
NO LO
PROPERTY

D0917442

UNEARTHING SECRETS
GATHERING TRUTHS

Jules Arita Koostachin

August 2018

Published by Kegedonce Press
11 Park Road
Neyaashiinigmiing, ON N0H 2T0
www.kegedonce.com
Administration Office/Book Orders
P.O. Box 517
Owen Sound, ON N4K 5R1

Printed in Canada by Ball Media
Cover Photo: Summer Faith Garcia
Back Cover Photo: courtesy of
J.A. Koostachin
Author Photo: Karolina Turek
Design: Chantal Lalonde Design

Library and Archives Canada Cataloguing in Publication

Koostachin, Jules Arita, 1972-, author
       Unearthing secrets / Jules Arita Koostachin; edited by Joanne Arnott.
— First edition.

Poems.
ISBN 978-1-928120-14-8 (softcover)

       I. Arnott, Joanne, 1960-, editor II. Title.

PS8621.O664U54 2018   C811'.6   C2018-903837-3

"God and Me" and "Kokoom" were previously published in The Willow's
Whisper: A Transatlantic Compilation of Poetry from Ireland and Native
America Edited by Jill M. O'Mahony and Mícheál Ó hAodha (Cambridge
Scholars, UK) 2011.

All rights reserved.
No part of this book may be reproduced in any form or by any electronic
or mechanical means including information storage and retrieval systems,
without permission in writing from the Publisher. Member of Access
Copyright Sales and Distribution – http://www.lpg.ca/LitDistco:

For Customer Service/Orders
Tel 1–800–591–6250 Fax 1–800–591–6251
100 Armstrong Ave. Georgetown, ON L7G 5S4
Email orders@litdistco.ca
We acknowledge the support of the Canada Council for the Arts which last
year invested $20.1 million in writing and publishing throughout Canada.

We would like to acknowledge funding support from the Ontario Arts
Council, an agency of the Government of Ontario.

RICHMOND HILL PUBLIC LIBRARY
3297200117412 9 RG
Unearthing secrets, gathering truths
Nov. 12, 2018

In dedication to the resilience
of *IsKweWak*

Unearthing Secrets
Gathering Truths

InNiNeWak

InNiNeWak – The Human Beings of MoshKeKoWok

MoshKeKo village	human	growing quickly	change approaching
short trees	human	generously spread	connection to land
gravel pathways	human	floating dust	bay side shacks

INNINEWAK

leaving home	people	lost youths	bright skyline
straight lines	people	concrete towers	invisible beings
guidance denied	people	cement barricades	questioning truths

INNINEWAK

resilient *KoKoom*	life	*MiTeWin* – dream	spiritual presence
deep bond	life	never broken	herstory
red *IsKwew*	life	silent cries	prayer

INNINEWAK

MoShoom	Cree	leather hands	aged tools
descendant	Cries	skilled hunter	trapper
four directions	Call	reclaiming	feeding souls

INNINEWAK

human
CRIES
dreaming

DANCING AATIMWAK

MINO KISIKOW

sun shining
tall blades of grass slice through me
reaching toward the other side
garbage scattered across the burnt yellow blades of once green
rusty shopping carts
traces of copper in the streams
walking through the knee-high bushes
finally breaking my way to nothingness

dancing *AaTimWak*
laughing at me from afar
haunting
tied back with ropes for no good reason
the forgotten beasts
unwanted
neglected by our disrespect for what once was
held back from roaming the swampy landscape
cowering from children who throw stones
both are undesirable
abandoned
we choose to ignore

the swamps host our paper shacks
held together with hammered plywood
sheltering Indians
baking Indian bread with raisins
some fry it too
bannock made with white powdery death
sugar
flour
salt
sizzling in animal fat
smokehouses and dried *WiYas*

dancing *AaTimWak*
watch our every move
each shack is our sanctuary
moldy temples
disconnecting us from one another
once rooted as a people
a distant memory reminding us
in a waking sleep
some roots are rotten
with sorrow
with secrets
poisoned

      dancing *AaTimWak*
      once our protectors
      guarding us from entering the dreams that are not our own
protecting the *InNiNeWak* – human beings – from where we have no
right to be
sad beasts
hold no place in the spirit world anymore
lost in the land of the living
waiting for us to find ourselves
long time coming

with deafening yelps
dancing rez *AaTimWak* keep reminding us
but we don't want to remember
with each sound they make they pull me deeper inside
back into their spirit bound world
tattered stories of our foremothers
memories are exhilarating

dancing *AaTimWak*
penetrating into my skin
with sharp teeth they drag me back
deep into the cavity of my being
I yearn to witness
to know the truth
who are we really?
seeing through me
am I a failure?
watchful eyes follow my every move
knowing my truth
I am invisible to myself
my ancestors are disappointed in me
the spirits are visible to *AatimWak*
eyes small and concentrated
leading me to the sacred spirit world

dancing *AaTimWak*
want us to listen
the protectors of our people
protectors of the moss
swamplands
joining us with the others
we need to cross through salty blue waters of the bay
follow behind them
trust them
seals and belugas will smile as we pass
back to my place
the *MoshKeKoWok* – my ancestral lands
we are rooted
generations before me gather
all beings speaking the same language

dancing *AaTimWak*
take me back home
soul needs to be fed
tired of not seeing
not listening
not being
feed me with the truth
feed me with *InNiNiMoWin* – my Cree language
I will dance with you
I will listen again

Memory from Long Ago

my world shifted for a moment
the past has come up to slap me in the face
ten years ago today
wolf was born
feeling alone and scared
pleading that the spirits would walk with me
looking into his little face
afraid to move through time with him

fragile young mother
father absent
his choice to leave
walking past me
seeing through me
invisible
my swollen belly
shamed, rejected

I remember
listening to the Pow Wow drums
relaxing my soul
resting my tired body
I sit
gathering my scattered thoughts
looking around at the people

elder sees me without really looking
shunning me
he thinks I'm white
he doesn't care about my swollen belly
hands shaking in my face
rejected again
horrible man
not my elder

feeling lost
swallowing the pain
lump in my throat
remembering hurts
powerful being
finding my path
through my son's guidance

shining light into my life
forgiving is hard
necessary
he teaches me
forgive those who smudge your soul he tells me
he is my teacher
always laughing
not afraid to remember

BATTLE

struggling with English words
how do you identify me?
you have no idea who I am
you cannot see beyond the flesh
only what you project onto me
your disappointment stings
creates a battle inside me

ATTACK

today seems to be the time of the enemy
life is swinging to one end of the pendulum
healing is delayed
once again we are waiting
not sure for what
drowned by the empty words of idiots
I question myself
what do I have to say?
does it matter?

PURPOSE

hard times ahead
hate revealing its ugly face
ignorance
stupidity in disguise
shutting me down
they are blind to the world in which we live
where we embrace our realities
we live in a place distant from the future

FAILURE

communities are filled with doubt
unsure of what to expect
today is timeless
countless actions of resistance
we continue to fight the monsters of humanity

RESULTS

minds and spirits on the battlefield
defeating only our selves
emotions held captive
safety from them
safety from us
the divide
bleeding into each other slowly

ENERGY

gods in the Earth
gods in the Sky
gods in the Wind
gods in the Stars
unattainable
proceed carefully
walk amongst each other with caution

SURVIVE

there are ones that judge
they are blinded by ego
trapped in hopelessness
forever reaching for what they will never have
they plead for freedom
from the shackles of expectations

TRUST

believe in the goodness of life
acknowledge the recognized
ask yourself who is genuine
living with intent
combating each day

HARMONY

ask what does liberty mean
what is freedom in a colonial world?
what is choice?
we always have to ask permission
even of ourselves

GOD AND ME

white man was my father
now I work for him
why am I here?
does Ma even know?
storytelling...
this story of Creation
is Jesus my God?
my mother is God!
my mother is very powerful
she can carry a child in her belly
in her belly!
all womyn
not W-O-M-A-N
w-o-m-y-n!
how do you spell it?

who will plant the seed in the earth
in Mother Earth?
a father?
who is my father?
why did he leave?
no respect for womyn

she loves to make love to men
but will she make love to herself?
does she know what love is?
she did once
in her innocence
bitch!
I'm sorry!
it's not your fault Mother Earth
shut Up!
because ceremony is lost
only to be found by the Seventh Fire
me
pressure!
I'm a lost light
in the dark with no identity...

a pissed off inner child
OChao!
that's me
a stupid lost fly
I'm caught in my future web

I'm here because of her
you kill a womyn and you kill a people!
mama
KoKoom
AsKi
PiSim

I asked the BIBLE to leave my heart to make new for the truth of my
identity

KiiiWayTeNook
WaPaNo
NaKaPayHaNook
ShaWaNook
NiiPii
IsKoTew
NoTin
AsKi

Mee'Kwetch
KiChi MaNiTo

Trapped in Freedom

trapped in a decaying school
battered dormitory
drowning child cries under water
barricade
transforms
death
trees
ceiling above
sky scattered
specs of light
tiled floor
rot
dirt

AsKi
holding me tight
reassuring
roots creating a blanket of ties back home

eyes cannot see
spirit knows
she is the one
keeping me in her place
her words slice into my core
black covered head
representative of a white god
scowling
leading me nowhere
hateful

AsKi holds the remains of my ancestors
decomposed
yet giving back
life awaiting birth
nurturing
reincarnation
next generation
InNiNeWak

one day soon
the gathering loved ones await
Elders, parents, Knowledge Keepers
children
children of the children

13

                                     existing between worlds
                                             guiding stars
                                     blood continues to flow
                         streams and rivers of my descendants
                       pushing themselves back into the ground
                                               becoming
                                               one beat
                                             just listen
                           you will be free from their nightmare
essence
trunks of the trees holding our stories safe
branches reaching out for sunlight
hands touching *AsKi*
roots digging deeper into her
unearthing our truths
                             land
                   hosting all life forms
                        skies cover
                        air flows
                   cleaning away the sickness
                        diseases purge
               washing away the painted whiteness
                                                  MasKwa
                                        mouth of the cave
                                 beside old brown *IsKwew*
                                MasKwa our Spirit Keeper
                                           acknowledged
                             warning us when danger is near
                                         embrace my power
                                        see yourself in me
                                             giving back
                                                    life

gifted from my Ancestors
gift of my Spirit
gift of my Body
gift of my Mind
braided into one
woven into balance
blood of *AsKi*

brown *IsKweWak* together
joining in chant
voices strong with battle
humming
singing the old songs
spirits are with me now
never left me

choosing to ignore
mama declares she was alone
in the darkness
praying to come home
blaming them
spirits walking with her
everyday
to the end of nothingness
every step of the way

blow to the stomach
flying back across the stillness of the lake
watching as the *IsKweWak* fade into the tree line
hoping to be with them
it is not my time yet
daughters
great granddaughters
hoping to hear the old stories
a little while longer

stories for future leaders
stories to guide
stories living in our Mothers
stories bleeding through our Grandmothers
Teachers
Fire Keepers
next generation
yet to be born
carrying the torch forward

across the waters
old brown *IsKwew* waits
KoKoom crawls out from the Sacred Lodge
lifting her head slowly
nakedness
IsKweWak side by side with eyes wide open

sisters
lovers
friends
family
community
standing in unison by *KoKoom's* side
                          another brown *IsKwew* free
                              revealing her face
                           erased from hardship
                                my mama
                      sadness she once carried
                              gone now
                   yet her past still haunts her
                 body now strong and healthy
               swollen curves of womanhood
                         beautiful
                          inhale
                  letting my breath go
                         breathe
                         breath
                         exhale
                     invigorating
                   pain released

                                                  gift of water
          NiiPii rushes over my feet sharing its sacredness
                        flowing into the stillness of the lake
                                  love for my mother
                                 drinking her gifts
                              cleansing her spirit
                                lake once dead
                               alive with life
                          her life is now her own
                                      finally

flash of light
shining down
rays of bright colors
lift my mama up
introducing her to Sky *IsKwew*
brown *IsKweWak* of the past
standing in soft darkness surrounding her
glowing

alive
soul once lost
mama's soul
gently descending from above
nourished with love
love falling into her
soul has returned to the shell
back from the long voyage
away

face to face
faced with the truth
staring into each other
seeing her for the first time in this life
in this form
knowing the spirit
mama speaks to me

sharing the language of the human beings
InNiNiMoWin

KoKoom

wrinkled brown face
eyes fill with story
five children lost
four buried

crosses held high
Jesus Christ!
nightfall
eyes glow
staring
sharp
judgmental
statue of Mary
white beads of their gods

respect the book
stinging wounds
war of faith
lost and found
souls burning
smoked hides
drying meat

walking the path
playing
touching
feasts of laughter
shameless dreams
forbidden thoughts

bingo dabbers
full speed
concentration
listen
quiet
BINGO!

leathery faces
soft touch
braids loose
oiled hair
bear grease
floral scarves
wrapped tight

ice crackling
cold snow

tinted yellow light bulbs
green walls
recycled dead wood
sewing machine
wingless flies
entrapped in a glass fortress

static
loud Cree voices
radio conference
one circular language
descriptive
white man politics
don't concern the Indian much

Longing: InNiNeWak Love Story

longing for your truth
still waiting for you
listening to the emptiness
bored of their talk
distracted by nonsense
looking up into the skies
stars gently place themselves upon the blue
darkness approaches from afar
threatening to overpower
teasing with lightning
clouds scatter
humiliated by the thunder
raw swollen flesh
reaches for the sky
wanting
needing
free me from dreaming
it will never be

longing to flood the Earth with my waters
flowing through my pores
exhaling into you
breathing deeply into myself
catching my breath with hope
find it before it's lost forever
trembling from my core
a veil of uncertainty wraps itself around me

longing for my fire within
my feet do not touch the ground
below me I fall
cold to touch
weightless darkness
floating down a footpath
I settle on a sandy beach
alone with myself
feeling watched
blackness of the rainwaters
seduction is tempting
taunting me
voices entangled in the trees
hearing me
whisper

longing for renewal
unraveling my sweet disorder
stench of rotten berries
stings my nostrils
choking on the taste
repelled
witnessing the flow
streams
veins of waters
spirit emerges
watchful eyes on me
hard panting from the bush
turning to see
paralyzed with devastation
no one is there

longing for your name
dancing with spirits
inside me
jolt of delight
penetrates
pushing its way through
down my spine
sweetness on my tongue
retreating inside
unbearable lust
impatient
washing away the hunger
chest pushes out
dream out loud
yearning
soul searching

longing to remember
sadness overcomes me
sultry days
leathery brown hands touching
radiant lights
shine

WaWaTae
shadows flee in fear
finding of self
cleaning my mouth of their foreign ideals
words that do not belong to my people
voices like tiny spiders
creeping their way out
escaping
open gap
teeth chattering
blood falls
screaming silence

longing for the mountain kiss
body surrenders
spinning in circles
face to face
trapped between
struggling to freedom
starving lightning strikes
await on the horizon for the right moment
swaying harmoniously
a bull charges
tracking me
fearful weeping
I turn away
not today

longing for the branches to brush the sky clean
darkness fades
eyelids slam shut
hint of your presence
sun breaks in
soul gently opens up
disappearing in you
arms stretched up
reaching for the Creator
I become Sky Woman

IsKwew

we are one
no longer trapped in the spruce
squirming
pulling away
pity prayer
my angered spirit leaves
unfed for too long
releasing me from its grasp
undeserving of my new fire
I burn
shedding the skin of the living
like a snake
I am renewed
longing to return to the dead

longing for your truth
I return to my original host
wait once again
abused being
honest
slamming hard against the softness of the swamp
I wake up
to the home of my ancestors
mysterious man stands over me
speaking in a tongue
I do not understand him
he is concerned
touching me
I rage
I never said you could
fingertips soft
caressing
bodies
convulsing to release

longing for your truth
I wait for you once again

WiKwam

WiKwam

IsKweWak
slowly emerging
tundra hugs their cold bare feet
absorbing the red soil
swallowing warmth
centering the being
walls tied together with sinew
intestine
leather becomes my veil
veil of red *AsKi*
Earth
camouflaging
protection
steering me away from the lies
untruths told
misleading stories of us
the human beings
MoshKeKoWok
InNiNeWak
standing tall
together
WiKwam

SHAKING TENT

red blood scarf
soft and long
wrapped around my head
keeping my hair in place

I enter the portal

gospel music
out of tune
no shame
our language consumes me
pulling me home
plummeting me back from the dreamland
back into the pew
I am now beside *KoKoom*
she prays under her breath
my heart hits hard against my armor of ribs
I want to get out of this place
church is not for me

Shaking Tent
heart thrashing
beating its way out of me
I take *KoKoom*'s hand in mine
we walk out the door
so this is sovereignty?
turning our back on their gods
returning to our own ceremonies
twirling about
euphoria
shaking tent sits abandoned
pleasured by our presence
it opens itself up to us
the passage to another dimension
Indian time machine
no present
no past
no future
multiple dimensions
peace
spirits rejoice
celebrate the return
singing aloud
we pray together

KoKoom and I
I am the seer
they embrace us
love
reclamation
we share this spirit place
no time or in-between
Indian Spirits
Little People
WinTiKo – Hungry Spirit
OChiSkwaCho – Sacred Being
Tricksters assemble
revealing truths
they tease
gossip about the living
drinking hot root tea
roots sweeten the water
mixing in lard with their long skinny digits
radio bingo blasting
belly laughs
feasting on bannock and berries
they play poker too
with cigarettes burning
smokes hanging from their drying lips
this is the gathering of the Shape Shifters

they have been waiting for our return
they are the Spirit Beings
speaking ageless words
ridiculing the living
as trauma pollutes our minds
mocking the English spoken by Indians
English is a disease they scream
it is spreading from generation to generation
poisoning the link to the ancient ones
disengaging us from the old stories
stories with life
our words are strong
once connecting the living with the dead
now what do they do?

KoKoom and I dream
we enter through the passage way
traveling through time and space
Shaking Tent Ceremony revived
Indian style
classy
resilience
exploring
we travel
witness the existence of other beings
Sky people
entire relations converse
there is no divide
nothing separates us from them
AaTimWak – dogs guard the portals
crows and ravens watch
revitalization
strength
KoKoom and I light the fire
burning
fire so big
flames lick the still air
red
orange
blue
for the living to see

CHILD UNDER WATER

walking along a path
sky darkened with clouds
a bridge lies ahead
afraid to cross
stopping myself
standing in the middle of the bridge
dirty obnoxious men
sit along the water's edge
filthy needles sinking deep into their arms
breaking through their skin
head thrown back
ecstasy
feeling the high
selfishly guarding
a child trapped under the water

anger shelters her
inner voice yells at me
save the little girl
the girl under the water
deep breathing
exhale slowly
become the warrior
stench of the men
gagging
poison is strong
prisoners of their addictions
I make it across
I am there near the water
I gently put my feet into the coldness
in the center of the stream
pulling the child up to my chest

her eyes closed
body limp
shaking her gently
slowly she wakes
screaming soundlessly
men watch
they move in closer
child is familiar
she is me...

I hold her close
crying out silently
the warmth of my body soothes her
she opens herself up to me

how did she stay alive under the water?
surviving for so long without breath

our eyes lock
she stopped breathing
a long time ago
I hold her so close
we become one again
we take a breath together
once again
she is finally free

men remember
children once trapped
pained by residential school
beaten
hurt
severed
move along now
it's time to go
it's time to live your lives
heal
be free

PAINED SPIRITS

dark fog slowly sweeps down
racing around the small pained spirits
mist encroaches upon their cores
smoky ghosts

water suddenly hardens
under my bare feet
changing
empty schoolyard

little brown children weep
Tree People once stood behind them
disappeared
now a dilapidated building stands

straining to see
searching the cracked windows
shadows staring from behind glass
whispering escape plans

loved ones await
body heavy
trying to run towards them
flight of moths scattering from my mouth

secrets hidden
freed with illegal Indian talk
fog swallows the children whole
they are gone

silhouetted trees
children who once were
sound of weeping
soul punctured

forgetting, not forgiven

WATCH AND WATCHED

faded paleness of clouded eyes
pink disgusting hard touch
hatred spilling from his gaping mouth
unexplained convictions
blaming me for his actions
abusive words slice through me
travelling to my gut
sticking to my spirit
I need to purge this memory
fragments of this memory
slowly burning my soul to black ash
torturous
it reminds me of deep sadness

watch from the false safety of glass barricades
no balance
faintly hear his barks of confusion
stupidity
he falls from grace
he will rise again
only more vulnerable
with no honour
he has no pride
his eyes penetrating
carving through my skin of deep pink
quickly his words turn to blood
thirsty
messiness
scattered
spitting nonsense at me with bullets of fluff
disassociate
I leave my shell
to my safety in the concrete walls

I watch with conviction
he is overwhelmed with lust and hatred toward me
I am a child
small and innocent
he is distant from the truth
isolation bleeding through a tired small hole
he wheezes
craving for control over me
I was born not too long ago

confusion sets in
he grasps chilled brown bottle
my presence triggers *WinTiKo*
eating my flesh
locking me in closets
threatening me
devouring my future

watching his lies unfold
his addictions laugh at his excuses
chilling memories of childhood
haunting blind eyes
they observe
they know
nothing stops this from happening
staring right through spirit
cheeks hot
bodies drained of color
feet heavy
soul defeated
as every day passes
I dig deeper into myself
hiding from this memory

I can no longer watch
finger bruised arms
stench of firewater
burning my hopes to nothingness
pulled into his foul smelling pollution
no more
I fight to fight
I dream to dream again
I want to tell someone
they won't listen to me
please hear my sadness
unlock the door
unleash me from his hold
I want to breathe again
I need to take myself back

LIGHT SWITCH

a gnawing ghastly voice
pressing through deafened ears
darkness circles
the touch of his pleasure
cold and empty air
released from his lips
pale with death
he sings alone
colourless memories
dreamless nights
music plays
he never feels the beat
disconnected

Light SWITCH
blackness
running
sensitive
alive
taste of apples on my tongue
KoKoom expectant
surrender to the safety of her arms
momentarily escaping

tied with his ugly truth
sickened world
my imagination no longer mine
haunted by unwanted visits
traces of his hand
pressed on my body
scarred
belly swollen in time
cellar door closes
slit of light under the dungeon gate
chapped red peeling mouth
hungry for my innocence

caressed
fallen into the depths of my meditation
chipped yellow painted house
wood stove burning
water boiling
bubbles rising
kettle whistling
sweet smell of red berries
return home

whispers of contentment
blinded by the opened door
familiar voice
run
freedom
running
wind in my face
the smell of apples on my breath
mouth quiet
closed
secrets

Transformation

pounding heart
breaking free
caged body
blood protected
foreign world
fire burning deep
smoke swirls out from my being
sweat drips from above
water stings my skin
rain twirls
seducing
darkness surrounds me
my head drops forward

transforming
shape shift
skin walkers
imprisoned behind wooden bars
alone on the sandy floor
mysterious man has gone
loneliness
soul urgently pushes out from the confines
bones and flesh

transform
I am a beaver
trapped in a wooden cage
I am a moose
trapped in the spruce
shooting pains
stabbing my gut
keeling over
a drop of rain
spirit spirals back down
into my human shell

transform
no longer a beaver
no longer a moose
inspecting my hands
they do not belong to me
they are dark
leathery
an old *IsKwew*
redness escapes
pores open
dripping into a lifeless lake
awakening the water spirits
the pain subsides

across the waters
old brown *IskWew* awakens
calling out to me
smiling warmly
eyes inviting me
cross over to the other side
she is plucking geese
she waits

transformation
great lodge stands
WiKwam of families
towering behind the old brown *IsKwew*
animals wander
in and out of the lodge
they walk together
they talk to each other
peaceful exchange
speaking to one another
I understand

Eyes Like Water

man with eyes like water
blue skies
towers over her
amused
weathered deep lines
pale colours
woven into his face
inquisitive
otherness
staring intensely through her eyes
spitting nonsense
commanding

she avoids his preying eyes
singing songs from a long time ago
travelling to a far away place
leaving the physical shell
spirit place
salty water drips onto her dry lips
songs soothing
reminder of home
opening her eyes
voice releases

MoshKeKoWok
lands of the foremothers
break her fall
far away from him
Sky *IsKwew* embraces us all
regardless
soft earth below awaits
her *KoKoom* appears
holding her tightly with strong arms
washing him away with her song
cleansing with *NiiPii*
song is strength
KoKoom embraces
voice soothes
across the lake of ancestors
our relations witness
the warriors

KoKoom lets go
sinking underneath
water shield
body heavy with his lies
she is not afraid
NiiPii hugs her softly
emerging
healing warmth of the *NiiPii*
she breathes again
reclaiming
resilience

KoKoom sings her an old song
releasing her

Battered Hope

silenced breathing
muffled screams
inhaling the black clouds of dust
violent pull into the red frosted *AsKi*

skin ripped
dragged into the bushes
Tree Spirits witness
rocks stabbing
dried mud underneath me
beaten down
hope

inconvenience to him
angered
it's gone too far
I'm in the way

black long tangled hair
wisps of pride
disassociation saving the soul
shadows transform

MasKwa's cave
hibernation
winter approaching
WinTiKo lurks

shivering from the cold
mouth of the dark hole
distorted open eyes
fear nothing
evilness hiding in the shadows

MasKwa exits the mouth
wickedness dissolves into shadow
vanishes into sky
nothingness fades

MasKwa hollers
warming me
body heat
saving me from a forgotten death

old brown man
kindred spirit
hunter and trapper
leather strong thick hands
a lean-to behind him
places his hands on my feet
grounding me
he prays to the ancestors

Nights of Seeing

voices loud
screaming at me
war
nights of seeing those who wander

whispers from the darkness
weight on my chest
pressing hard
sleeping torn

waking in a fury
sun shines through my window
gasp in relief

SHAPE SHIFTER

Earth gently finding its way under my toes
sand cold
refreshing
I play
spinning round and round
arms stretched out

smells fill my nostrils
sweetness of nature
MasKwa watches

MasKwa shoves me with its warmth
wet nose tickling
breath in my face
seeking refuge

soft brownness
tiny
insignificant
reassurance
safety

MasKwa tumbles down
transformation begins again
empty black fur at my feet
soulless now
gone
traveling afar
through dimensions

underneath me
movement
possessed by spirit
leaving my skin behind too
piled below me
like dirty laundry
piled high with all my dark memories
I shed the weight of my shell
Shape Shifter

lovely
skin glistening in the remaining sunlight
sparkling lake
lights the sky
warm summer breeze

IsKweWak watch from a distance
opening their doorways
too far away
across the blue of waters
lodge stands
sacred *IsKweWak* spirit home
InNiNeWak IsKweWak
all ages standing together
holding each other's hands
heads lowered
chanting
praying
singing to me

fear explodes from within
anxiety
were they always there?
at the sacred home?
waiting
watching me

lifting my eyes to the sky spirits
clouds still
home rocks back and forth
leather flap bursts open
steam escapes
meeting the cool air
from the darkness
naked *IsKweWak* crawls out
legs strong
black loose hair
covering
brownness
slick with sweat
eyes lifted

spirit name whispered
confused I listen
ancestors speaking
through the Tree Spirits
inside the bush of the swamps

I am forced by their love to look forward
IsKweWak fade away
No! MoNa! No!
I slam back into the pile of skin
all the memories of this life remind me of who I am
gasping for air
I cry
I feel lost again

I stop
I listen
I open my heart
I hear them

they still sing for me
they still pray for me
they are still there for me

MiTeWin

MiTeWin

one night I dreamt hard
I was lying on the beach
sandy feet below
sun scorching my skin
Earth beneath
holding me up to the skies
hot air
melt
melting deep
deeper and deeper
inside myself I find her

enjoying the voices
loving the feeling
calm softness
wanting home
melting deeper
falling inside myself
to the center of my brown shell
swallowing me whole
tasting everything sacred
absorbing my soul

take me back
set me free from nightmares
and keep the spirits away from my sleep
return me whole
not fragmented
but take a bit from the sky
fill me up
and steal a little from the oceans
take all parts of me too
and touch the Goddess
so she can crave me
one night I dreamed hard

Stolen Cubs

creek swells
grey furious clouds
filling the black sky
feet chilled from the frosted red Earth
pathways no longer cleared
footprints of the stolen disappear

MasKwa IsKwew shows herself
pleading
mourning loss
pups thieved
dragged from her breasts
she cries
placing my hand on *MasKwa*'s head
gently comforting her
no words
desperate *MasKwa IsKwew* runs
toward the Tree People

MasKwa IsKwew sways with every step
belly still swollen with new life
milk drips down toward the cold Earth
underneath her she drinks
pleading with the witnesses
Tree People shamed
attempt to pacify
whispering to her
sorry
sorry
sorry
MasKwa IsKwew does not hear them

Tree People are angry too
no words of comfort
nurturers of the stolen
harsh wind
swirling around
lifting me
up into the sky
I fall
detached
drifting
searching the forest

where are the stolen?
old *IsKwew* waits
the other side of the waters
red lake ice-covered
time prevents
something broke in the *MasKwa*
something broke in the *InNiNeWak* too
old *IsKwew* prays for the return of the stolen

clearing in the bush
old school decrepit
just a shell
weak spirits of the stolen perform
white men with faces hidden
watching from the crevices
guarding the stolen souls
the stolen pray
a god of another place
frightened

despair
families
holding hands
forming circles
around the grounds of the undead
hoping with heads bowed
chants deafening
piercing
beings of the swamp wake
Earth shakes

old twisted
Tree Person
bare
naked
nearly dead
the stolen sit
exposed roots
hollowed eyes begging
the stolen dream of home
dreaming of *KoKoom* and *MoShoom*
Mama
Papa
Tree Person reaches down
kisses the tops of their heads with flowered fingertips
exhales the last of life

roots wrapping themselves around the stolen
stories preserved in the Earth
the land of their ancestors
they will never be forgotten
children put to rest
with love
closing eyes
remembering home

families circle each other
saying their last words
asking the ancestors to embrace their children
resilience

Possessed

man stands on the tracks
face grotesque
missing girl lies at his feet
chest carries a gaping hole
a heart was once there
blood stains his mouth
red stains his hands
he was feasting on her soul
eyes are dark
evil
soul possessed

twin girls beside him
run!
voice drained
only silence
standing at either side of him
twins troubled
WinTiKo cannot see them
innocence obscured
lightness encircles
twins protected

brown *IsKwew* in the forest
tilting her head
warning
motionless
sinew tied around her
animal intestine
rope

reaching for my mouth
mouth sewn shut
needle box
paralyzed
helpless
I witness

WinTiKo yelps
language of death
greed
hunger
unrecognizable
wanting and tasting the brown *Iskwew*
grabbing at her
desirable
necessary to exist
belligerent
combative
hostile
fights
refusing to be its next victim
brown *IsKwew* digs her nails
draws blood from the undead
powerless

hands touching my bare back
throwing me down
onto the softness of the Earth
MoShoom follows
unnoticed
touching swollen ankles
releasing me from the pain
MoShoom whispers calmly
he tells me to let go

NaPaw
NaPaw
NaPaw

sleep
sleep
sleep

brown *IsKwew* gone
in her place I stand
at the mercy of the *WinTiKo*
stinks of death
rot
long wiry claws
holding me prisoner
heart beats
drumming against my ears
brown *IsKwew* gone
twins sit side by side
on the tracks waiting
faces once gaunt
skin now healthy
pink

MoShoom
brown *IsKwew*
walking out of the bushes
twins saunter over toward them
exhilaration
embraced by parents
I call out to them
no one sees me
MoShoom turns
only for a moment
he has to leave
MoShoom leaves without me

MasKwa
exiting the mouth of the cave
my body on the cold rock
WinTiKo screams out at *MasKwa*
cautioning
MasKwa charges *WinTiKo*
WinTiKo surrenders

brown *IsKwew*
encirclement
back on the tundra
acceptance
quietness
restful
I let go
again

Mourning Song

alone I exist
body rests hovering above the water
dark lake imprisons me
my shell floats towards the shores of isolation
sky above
streaked with gold and silver
watchful spirits
mourning loss

IsKwew lies motionless
beneath the waters
held down
bottom of the lake
seaweed
keeping her in place
dead eyes
fixed
IsKwew's belly swollen
life lives within her rotted womb

beating heart of the unborn
penetrates eardrum
IsKwew's black loose hair
circles around her starved body
two long braids flow
beautifully around her oval sunken face
eyes pleading with mine
she slowly reaches for me

IsKwew's wrists are tied with sinew
bare chest holds a wound
dark hole no longer bleeds
mouth opens
afraid to hear
her trauma is mine
I turn away from her
sadness
strong *IsKwew*
once was

feet planted
standing still
watching her from the edge of green
distorted face
man appears
large white hands
stained with the blood of *IskweWak*
distorted face man disappears into the ground below
swallowing his hatred
Earth spits him out
repulsed
annoyed
disturbed

WinTiKo
cannibal spirit takes form
desiring human flesh
flesh of *IsKweWak*
her strength threatens him
feeding off fear
he attacks
WinTiKo eats
without remorse
disguises itself as man
living a lifeless life in lies
lives amongst us
cannibal spirit
wandering the lands

MasKwa spirit
half bear and half man appears
Tree People release *MasKwa* spirit
to protect *IsKweWak*
MasKwa spirit approaches
weary of *WinTiKo*
not afraid
nostrils opening and closing
smelling the blood that stains the Earth
large brown head hangs low
swaying
sniffs around

MasKwa's piercing eyes
small and black
razor sharp teeth
ready to defend
devour
MasKwa spirit warns of the lurking *WinTiKo*
"*WinTiKo* is hungry again," *MasKwa* says
hungry for the souls of *IsKweWak*

brown *IsKweWak* crawl out
from the sand beneath
I witness this all
curious, I stay present
MasKwa's eyes redden
blood drips from my privates
swollen belly
I am her
emptied of life
infant spirit
entangled at my feet
spirit is an *Iskwew*

drum beats from the Earth's middle
beaten, abused
angry brown men stand
MasKwa finds me
digging me out from the sand
infant spirit untangled
she wants to stay with the brown *IsKweWak*
infant spirit waits till it is safe to breathe

MasKwa pulls me free
places my emptied body on the train tracks
tracks beside my *KoKoom*'s home
my body lies heavy
hidden from the *WinTiKo*
calling out for *KoKoom*
wetness fills my mouth
choking on my blood

KoKoom's little yellow house with green trim
empty and alone
crying out song
home wants me to sing the ancient songs
I sing out
wood smoke fills the void in my belly
Wind Spirit enters
filling my chest with breath
heartbroken
pain is not only mine

MasKwa spirit approaches cautiously
pushes me with his long nose
embraces me
letting go
walks away
much more work to do

alone I exist
sky turns dark
metal of the train tracks strap me down
sucking the air out of my lungs
crows flying over me
Tree People whimper
Maskwa turns around
witnesses
I am afraid

sacred spirit
Backward Hands crawls out
warned of its presence
lives under the tracks
Backward Hands scurries about
eyes glaring
full of madness
hatred
face white
teeth curled up over its upper lip
sharpens its teeth
rubbing up against the train tracks
evilness
death spews at me
creeps toward me like a white man's demon
death is near

Backward Hands refuses to forgive
mother needs to be forgiven
forgive *KoKoom* for sending her away
four generations of *IskWeWak*
come together for ceremony
mind clears
breathing

Backward Hands speaks nonsense
distracting me from the truth
voice is here somewhere
I am the only one to find it
I need to free the *IsKweWak*
pained
pray in *InNiNiMoWin*
language of the human beings
TapWeWin
free *IsKweWak*

Breaking free from the tracks
I listen
IsKweWak tell me their stories
I am alive with their stories
return their memories home
weaken the *WinTiKo* with the guidance of their spirits
time to return home

wake with the sun
another day
warm breeze
remember the *IsKweWak*
tell their stories

Between Dreams

travelling to Poland
concentration camp
shattered by their stories
saddened by the pain of the place
spirits trapped
I pray for them to find peace
they are so full of grief
indignity and sorrow
my heart is aching
suffering
remorse

exhausted
I lie my head down on my pillow
soft and clean
mind racing
alone for the first time since arriving
darkness swallows me
but only for an instant
dream state transpires
consoled by the tiny specs of light
embraces me
calmness

a woman with a shaven head
she lies her head on my pillow
staring into me
deeply
I smile at her
she mirrors my movements
eyes large and brown
young beautiful face
who was she?
mouth small and pink
she smells both sweet and sour
clothes faded and tattered
her face gaunt
I am not frightened of her
she reaches out to me gently
do you see me?
behind her
shadows emerge from the blackness
vulnerable skeletons of what once was

spirits whispering
pale skin
hollow shells
once free to live
lost
memories
lost
first a few
then hundreds
thousands loom around me
reaching for the life they once had
yearning to be remembered
but forgotten
melancholy

broken
her eyes shut hard
cutting through me
settling my mind
peacefulness through the shadows
remember the forgotten ones
deafening tears
the woman leans in
presses her lips onto mine
tears are warm
she becomes me
I become her
we are one

DEATH DREAM

in my dream I am home alone
a stranger barges in
he raises his gun
no time to run
the bullet pierces through my head
my body is heavy
pain is excruciating
pain subsides
I die
this is death?
my soul escapes my shell
time no longer exists

I wake in the Spirit World
I am running from something
but no one is behind me
I panic
my hallway is bare
it is still my house
but the house is empty
echoes
it feels endless
I am lost in my own home
the familiar voices of my family are faint
I am restless
I am searching
where is everyone?
how do I find them?

I hear crying from the basement
I find my way down
brown children line up
they are the undead
sorrowful
there is a large hole in the wall
a cellar
a different dimension
faces pleading with me
help me!

stop!
do not go into the darkness!
I am here
please just wait for the song
the living will sing for us
they will help us find our way out of here

blank stares
I am frightened
no one sings
we wait
one by one they enter the hole in the wall
a girl with a distorted face stares through me

I wake
these souls need our prayers
we need to sing our old songs
we need to wake the trapped children
we need to remember them

FACELESS FIGURES

dark figures
visiting from the blackness
standing very still
listening to my song
closer and closer
they are brave
many shadows
surround my bed

silhouettes
never faces
heart beats quickly
look away
night visits
every night I wait
seeing past my soul
they stare

pressing down on my chest
Spirit Keepers
help me
the visitors are frightening
they mean no harm

they play tricks
my doll possessed
fearing the sun setting
darkness falls
sleeping with eyes open

sharing their stories in my dreams
haunting me
fleeing as the sun rises

I can see them
planting themselves at the foot of my bed
watching me
go away!
they fade into the darkness
yet still present in spirit
dark figures with no eyes
visitors with faded faces

lights out
panic sets in
never asking my permission
running free
stalking me
wanting to be heard

walking the line
life and death
gift of sight they say
others choose not to see
faceless figures
waiting to be heard

time passes
no fear anymore
annoyed at times
I have set boundaries
but now they visit my children

Murdered

MURDER

news of his death

MURDERED

lost for words

OVER

overwhelmed

PAST

not present

DEMONS

giving up

PAIN

alcohol and drugs

DIFFICULT

anger and disappointment

LIFE

hearts heavy

AGONY

fighting with recovery

FREEDOM

left to die

SPIRIT WORLD

his resting place

PEACE

HOME

heart sinks deep inside my cage of ribs
picking up the lost pieces
fragments sucked in with every breath
stop the drum for a moment

death taunts me
an urge to escape my container of flesh
desire to disappear into the blueness of sky
surrender to the earthquake of spirits

laid down
man ignores the world in which I exist
finding a corner in my mind
music swirls like a lullaby

the quiet lonely
searching for life within
digging holes in my skin
need to feel alive

heart safe
within the cage of ribs
picking up the lost pieces
fragments woven together with every breath

drum beats
new life
container of flesh
protects me

IsKweWak

IsKweWak

voices release
soft tundra of my foremothers
Sky *IsKwew* surrounds me
Earth below
encircled
cloud

KoKoom
bring me to the *NiiPii*
towards the old brown *IsKweWak*
across the lake
whittling wood
tell them I have arrived

ceremony
doorway
words
watch me from above
distorted *NiiPii* separates us
I still feel her
no longer can I touch her

red scarf wrapped
hair of grey
cold frigid lake
KoKoom leans over
searching
finding

changing form
body frozen in time
ice shattering
breaking
reclaiming
old *IsKwew* sings
KoKoom sings

worlds become one
share my body
Ceremony unites
Spirit

Roots

my teachings tell me to leave the roots in the ground
never let them dangle
be strong in who you are
know where your roots come from
be proud of the people before you
listen to the spirits even when they are quiet
be aware
spirits are always around
try to be kind
be respectful when people are hurting

shed your skin every few years
detach
know your destination
continue on with love
say *Mee'Kwetch* for your endurance
never be fearful of change
interfere when you need to
discard people who only want to hurt you

my teachings tell me to be confident
live life with purpose
have courage
humility is key
speak your own truth
listen well
hear without interrupting

watch your back
be present
believe in something
have faith
know your teachings
live your teachings

Uncontrolled Concept of Time

milk
dripping and full
unborn child pushing down
alone she sits waiting
listening from the open world

crying from the circle of black
enclosed in the silence
warm fluid
crossed
cramped

mother's tears
widened space
dreams of colour
mood swings

sucking little thumb
tail attached
veins of blue and purple
eyes wide
muffled sounds
constrained

legs stretched
clarity
freedom
waiting
uncontrolled

uncontrolled

I Follow Behind

hundreds of miniature killer whales

swim in harmony

newly born human infant

swimming with a family of whales

an umbilical cord pulls a child

through the watery path

I follow behind

MOTHERHOOD

push   cry   fall   fail   guilt   love   forgive tired   push

circle of fire

Asivak
my son *OtTaNaFayCaSo* the spider

Mahiigan
my son the wolf

TapWeWin
my son the truth speaker
PaWaKen
my son the totem
NiiSoTeWak – Twins

AaShaNee
many daughters
good spirits
passed on

kisses from the Creator
passing of souls
through me

I am mother

Asivak

I was a young mother
birthing a new life
his eyes open
black circles of curiosity
intense and intelligent
already worried and responsible
cares for his family
wanting only the best
proud of his heritage
refuses to stand with the enemy
listens to all the stories
inner force strong
love emanates through him
needs to laugh
needs to dance
he is my son
my first-born
my savior
I was young and naive
but I loved his spirit
he was mine to protect
mine to love
so young
I did not fully understand my role
made many mistakes
but forgiveness is vital
mother guilt can kill the soul
the potential
the greatness of his being
so much to offer to this world
determination
part of the seventh generation
strong Inuk *InNiNew* being
he weaves the web of life all around him
my son, the Spider

Mahiigan

born second
a free spirit
protector
gentle
articulate
love feeds his spirit
always beautiful
born with his eyes closed
resilient sense of being
lives life without worry
buries himself in lots of hugs and kisses
he laughs out loud
belly laugh from the gut
deep sleeper
contented person
affectionate
compassionate
cares with all his heart
attached
smiles big and wide
happiness lives in his soul
true gift of selflessness
good intentions
naturally bright
spirited
always by his brother's side
never turns his back
helper
leader of the pack
fearless
adventurous
healer
Anishnabe InNiNew being
a good son
my son, the wolf

One Who Is Looking

spirits call her by name
one who is looking
uncovering teachings
learning to live in the present
not in a world that is yet to exist
poisoning the natural process of life

mama
mother of *AShaNee*
mother of Spider
mother of Wolf
mother of Truth
mother of Totem

shedding of the last *IsKwew*
who wore my moccasins
I no longer host her
the one who is looking
she rests now

walking into the light
step by step
finding bravery
new purpose

I become
IsKwew who holds *IsKoTew*

MAMA

Chi *Mee'Kwetch* mama
courageous actions silenced by them
yet your eyes have spoken for you
through me

reversed roles
words quieted
I was your voice
never a child
but that's okay

desperately trying to find a place
a place for the both of us
in this world
where you were afraid to defend yourself

stomach swells in sickness
I remember your defeat
every day I watched
your hurt became mine
anger and shame too
humiliation passed on to me

small trembling hands
always reaching for your closed fists
burning holes in me
I am not your enemy
I am your daughter mama
I just want your love

left alone
emptiness closing in around me
sinking deeper into myself as each day passed
where are my teachings?
I need a light mama
show me the way

grief is swallowing us
expelling us
why do you hurt me so?
I find it hard to ask you

haunting childhood memories
frightening glimpses into your past
disconnected
say something to me mama!
I need to forgive you
your prayers only last so long
take control mama
I don't want to give up on you

torn in many directions
it seems I am lost at every turn
except now I am a mother
I'm the mother of many sons
mama, did you know they chose me?
that must mean I am on the right track

Spirit told me we all have a right to choose
we choose before our first breath of life
why me though?
left wondering
am I a good mother to my sons?

afraid to speak like you
but I do
haunted by your fragmented memories
silenced by your fear
everything seems safe deep inside
where no one can reach

horrible secrets trapped
angering you
hints of the truth
words slip out

I needed protection
didn't I deserve to be protected?
you turned away
I held onto the promise of you
I'll help you fight the demons
we can do this together

your path in life was covered in debris
mine was as well
mama, I love you
I now know what you survived
I chose you from the spirit world, mama!

Nanan

small aged body
lying helpless
fetal position
barely holding her knees to her chest
elderly women sit around her
we wait
no one comes
empty wheel chairs
echoes of whispers
praying to the spirits
sharing with the ones they once knew
memories
shadows walk the corridors
waiting for her last breath

lines deep
eyes fading
hanging on to the world she was once a part of
strong in her past
vulnerable now
waiting for care as a child would

remembering her hair
once long and black
brown sweet face
hands soft
securely holding me
still resting my head on her chest
please don't leave me Nanan
who will I be without you?

will I still be me if you leave?
I want to follow her into the spirit world
longing for her to return
returning to us as she once was
through the next generation
spirits creep closer and closer
gently pulling her to the world of ghosts
world of memories
I beg for more time
How do I live without you?

the room has an odor of life drained
eyes are empty
each second that passes
death approaches inch by inch
sore tired bodies
lost minds
trapped in the past
reaching with broken hearts
for someone

piano playing
faintly heard
old people clapping
forgotten warriors
full lives
will this nightmare end?

once strong and free
locked down
fragile bodies
soft cries from the dark hallway
fallen
scared
exhausted
wishing for youthfulness
lost in regrets

I leave her there
abandoned
she watches me leave
Nanan knows I love her
I ignore my thoughts
I make myself believe
I will see her again
it's over
last day of her life as my Nanan

tears escape her sad eyes
my heart pains
heaviness
please no
stay with me Nanan

life stops

creator punches a hole through me
emptiness
pain like no other
I can't breathe
void

bye my Nanan
WatChia
no word for goodbye in our language
till we meet again
I love you

MoShoom

he was a son
brother   partner   father
he was a grandfather
he was a great-grandfather
a leader
he was a descendant
now he is an ancestor
his spirit with us still
he was a hunter
an *OkiMaw*
northern swampland was his home
he suffered tragedy
he was a silent survivor
the strongest person I know

he had leathery dark brown hands
short black hair   combed to the side   greased back
he wore black trousers
his legs were short and bowed
people called him *APiKoChish*
his back was always straight
dress shirts with suspenders
sat with legs stretched out in front of him
he liked listening to the radio
he only spoke *InNiNiMoWin*

he liked to bead moccasins with my *KoKoom*
he rarely smiled
but chuckled from the belly
he had gentle soft eyes
always watched over his family
he was a proud soul
he was a keeper of *InNiNeWak* knowledge
he carried the cross of a foreign religion
not known to his ancestors
he had dignity
he had faith in god
later in life he reclaimed the old ways
InNiNeWak medicines
he was a stubborn Cree man

nearing the end of his life as *MoShoom*
he sat alone and talked to himself
observing the changes around him
not seeing us
not hearing us
I guess he knew
the end was near

he liked being in his room
kissing his loving partner
caressing her hair
stroking her cheek
kissing her softly
they were so similar
together their whole lives
he comforted her
even after many years together
they still loved each other

he had so much pride
he stopped helping hands
only allowing the very young to play near him
they tumbled about
always stealing his cane
I was envious
I watched them all the time
he loved his great-grandsons
he was my *MoShoom*

LITTLE CREE GIRLS

summer in the north
with grandparents
small Native village
where horse flies bite
leaving life-long scars
hot sun burns
browning the skin

a little Cree girl with curly black hair from next door
introduces herself
her face pained
I can tell Cree girl has a heavy heart
many secrets
she plays with me anyway

Cree girls skip
Cree girls chase frogs
Cree girls love one another

I am the Cree girl with blonde hair
almost innocent
happy being with my *KoKoom*
although I've been hurt too
I have a playful spirit
I have a few secrets
yet to understand them
we are best friends
every visit I look forward to seeing her
every visit she waits for my arrival

one summer day
a man calls out from a dilapidated shack
I've been warned predators hunt up here
so we ignore the man
but I am curious
I want to investigate
little Cree girl with black curly hair pushes me down hard
I am confused
I wonder why
I don't understand why she wants to hurt me

the man calls out again
we ignore him a second time
the man yells louder at us
scaring us
I look at her
she is a protector
she knows what to do
even at the age of seven

Cree girl screams at me
pushing me down again
she sends me home
telling me she hates me
I want to stay with her
but she refuses to listen
I can't hold back the tears

we stare at each other
the man approaches us
she pushes me down again
screaming at me
her face is red and desperate
I leave my friend with the yelling man
it feels wrong
something tells me to stay to protect her
I turn to her
I cry
she pushes me again
this is the last time I see her

we lost touch so many years ago
I still think about her
nearly forty years later
I find my lost friend
the last day together still haunts us

she reveals a horrible truth
she saved me that day
I ask her why
what happened?
what did that man do?

I am heavy hearted as I listen
the little Cree girl knew what the man was going to do
she sent me away to save me from him

confused
we cry together

I ask her why
at such a young age she put me before herself

she tells me
I was the only light in her life

Returning to the Tracks

regrets haunt
childhood full of uncertainty
train tracks leading out to the world
a world where everyone is happy
nothing bad ever happens over there

Moosonee is a small place
the last stop
little brown hands waving at strangers on the train when it pulls in
eager to hear new stories from the white folks

my feet touch the tundra
I run on the dusty road
shoes covered in thick mud
flesh eating black flies biting hard

children hiding under the bridge
playing in the copper creek
taxi boats expecting white passengers
dogs running with no home
puppies looking for a master
harassing people until stones are thrown

northern store selling the basic necessities
top dollar
expensive as hell
living in what white man calls poverty
saying hello to known strangers as we pass by each other
visiting friends and family
what's the latest gossip?
smell of wood burning in the night
fills the air

WaWaTae
reaching across the horizon
black treetops
stars falling
sounds of animals
lurking in the bush
watching us
old ones calling children inside
little shack at the end of the gravel road
KoKoom waiting for me to return
running into her arms
holding *KoKoom* tight
I will never let her go
feeling secure
she is my medicine pouch
I am complete with her

MoShoom works in the shed out back
cool wind drops
late morning approaches
beams of light
dust floats down to the floor
my brothers and I stack cards with our crazy fun cousins
pure happiness
grandparents love us unconditionally
affection and encouragement

city life with mama
sad
lost connections
living with her untamed monsters
missing my grandparents
separated by distance
never comfortable here in the city
too much space between *KoKoom* and me

returning to the tracks
many years later
my children may never know
families now scattered
people alone in the city
living bare life
memories of the tracks make me smile
I still see her there
scarf wrapped around her head
her shack gone
memories of *KoKoom* warming our tea on the wood stove
MoShoom preps for his next hunting trip
the best
smell of smoked hide
stretching it with *KoKoom*
prepping it for moccasins
praying and laughing with *KoKoom*
not sure what we're praying for
being with her is heaven
I don't need anything else
we cook wild *WiYas*
teasing
I don't like wild *WiYas*

MoShoom dances to an old country song on the radio
if you're lucky he will pull out his accordion
laughter fills the night
bannock and tea
freshly picked sweet berries
playing radio bingo
hugs and kisses
peaceful sleeps
this is home
by the tracks
Moosonee

Glossary

MoshKeKo Cree (Swampy Cree)

AaShaNee – Good spirit
AaTimWak – Dogs
APiKoChish – Mouse
Asivak – Spider
AsKi – Land
InNiNew – Person
InNiNeWak – People (human beings)
InNiNiMoWin – Language of the Human Beings
IsKoTew – Fire
IsKwew – Cree womyn
IsKweWak – Cree Womyn
KiChi MaNiTo – Great Spirit
KiiWayTeNook – North
KoKoom – Grandmother
MasKwa – Bear
Mee'Kwetch – Thank you
MiNo KiSiKow – Beautiful day
MoNa – No
MoshKeKoWok – Ancestral lands of the Swampy Cree
MoShoom – Grandfather
NaKaPayHaNook – West
NaPaw – Sleep
NiiPii – Water
NiiSoTeWak – Twins
NoTin – Wind
OChao – Fly (bug)
OChiSkwaCho – Sacred being
OKiMaw – Leader/boss person
PaWaKen – Totem
PiSim – Moon/Sun
ShaWaNook – South
TapWeWin – Speaking truth
WaPaNo – East
WatChia – Hello/goodbye
WaWaTae – Northern Lights
WiKwam – Home
WinTiKo – Cannibal spirit
WiYas – Meat

About the Author

Born in Moose Factory Ontario, Jules Arita Koostachin was raised by her Cree-speaking grandparents in Moosonee, and also with her mother in Ottawa. Her mother is a survivor of the Canadian Residential school system. Jules is a band member of Attawapiskat First Nation, Moshkekowok territory, and she currently resides in Vancouver. She is a PhD candidate with the Institute of Gender, Race, Sexuality, and Social Justice with the University of British Columbia – her research focus is Indigenous documentary. In 2010, she completed graduate school at Ryerson University in Documentary Media where she received the Award of Distinction for her thesis work, as well as the Graduate Ryerson Gold Medal for highest academic achievement. While pursuing her Masters, Jules finished her first feature length documentary film, *Remembering Inninimowin*, about her journey of remembering Cree. After graduation, Jules was one of six women selected for the Women in the Director's Chair program at the Banff Center in Alberta, where she directed a scene from her feature script *Broken Angel*, currently in development. Jules' television series *AskiBOYZ* (2016) co-produced with Big Soul Production is about two urban Cree youth reconnecting with the land. *AskiBOYZ* is currently being aired on Aboriginal Peoples Television Network.

Over the years, Jules has established herself within the film and television community. Her company VisJuelles Productions Inc. has a number of films and other media works in development. In 2017, she released her short documentary *NiiSoTeWak* with CBC Short Docs and also *Butterfly Monument* with her co-director/producer Rick Miller. Jules was also the 2017 Aboriginal Storyteller in Residence with the Vancouver Public Library. Planet In Focus invited Jules as the lead filmmaker to work with Cree youth in Attawapiskat First Nation where they made over twenty films. In the fall of 2018, Jules is releasing a short narrative film entitled *OChiSkwaCho*. She is also in development with her television series *Threshold with Jules Koostachin*. She's presently working on two manuscripts, *Soul Kept* and *Moccasin Souls* about intergenerational resilience. She is lead editor and contributor of a forthcoming collection entitled *Children of Survivors* with the University of Regina Press. Jules carries extensive knowledge working in Indigenous community in several different capacities providing support to Indigenous women and children who face barriers; these community experiences continue to feed her advocacy and her arts practice. *Unearthing Secrets, Gathering Truths* is her first book of poetry, and was a twenty year journey.